ALL
HINDU TEMPLES

SWAMI HARSHANANDA

RAMAKRISHNA MATH

SRI RAMAKRISHNA MATH
MYLAPORE :: :: MADRAS-600 004

Published by
Adhyaksha
Sri Ramakrishna Math
Mylapore, Chennai-4

Total number of copies printed before 48,200

XV-2M 3C-2-2011
ISBN 81-7120-085-0

Printed in India at
Sri Ramakrishna Math Printing Press
Mylapore, Chennai-4

PREFACE

(to the first edition)

Much has been written on the Hindu temple. If some writers have meticulously traced its evolution through the ages, others have marvelled at its architecture and the engineering skill of its builders. A few have struggled to discover its meaning and symbology. But none of these writings keeps the average Hindu in view and supplies him with all the essential information in nontechnical terms. This is exactly what has been attempted in this monograph.

It may be a tall claim to say that it speaks "all about" the Hindu temples! But a little patient and sympathetic perusal will convince the readers that it is a modest attempt at providing essential information about the Hindu temple in a nutshell to a layman.

A few ideas that may help activate the temple and its dynamic rehabilitation in the Hindu society have been presented in the epilogue. It is hoped that these ideas will provide the modern Hindu leaders with some food for serious thought.

S.H

ACKNOWLEDGEMENTS

I am deeply indebted to Sri. K. Sitārāma, Somayaji, Professor of Saivāgama, Maharaja Sanskrit College, Mysore and Swami Śivapriyānandaji with whom I held discussions and clarified my doubts.

Sriyuts R. Narayana, B. C. S. Narayan, M. Ram Mohan and K. H. Rajagopala Reddy have contributed towards the blocks thereby helping the institution to reduce the price of the book. My grateful thanks to them.

My thanks are also due to Sri. R. Narasimha of the Samskrita Sahitya Sadana, Mysore, who has taken a personal interest in the neat printing and get up of the book.

S.H.

PREFACE

(to the second edition)

It is highly gratifying to note that all the 2,000 copies of the first edition have been sold out within 18 months. This shows that the book has fulfilled a long-felt need of the educated Hindus.

In the light of the criticism offered by scholars and reviewers, the second chapter embodying the brief history of the Hindu temples has been rewritten. The drawing also have been revised.

I am grateful to Prof. S. Srinivasachar of our RIMSE (Mysore-20) who has assisted me in this. I am also grateful to Sri. B. Ramappa of Replica Offset Printers, Bangalore who has taken a personal interest to produce the cover-jacket for the book. Sri. R. Narasimha of the Samskrita Sahitya Sadana has done a good job this time also in printing the book. My hearty thanks to him.

I hope that revised edition will prove to be even more popular than the first edition.

The spiralling of prices has necessitated the raising of the price of the book slightly. It is hoped that the readers will bear with the publishers.

S.H.

CONTENTS

		Page
1.	Introduction	1
2.	A Brief History of Hindu Temples	2
3.	Symbology of the Temple	9
4.	Construction of a Temple—Typical Steps	15
5	Essential Parts of a Typical Temple	20
6.	Iconography	23
7.	Religious Rites and Ceremonies	26
8.	Temple Arts and Crafts	30
9.	The Temple and the Devotee	31
10.	The Temple and the Priest	33
11.	The Temple and the Society	34
12.	Epilogue	37
13.	Index	53

LIST OF ILLUSTRATIONS

Fig. 1. Ground plan of a typical complex.

Fig. 2. Plan and elevation of the garbhagṛha, antarāla and maṇṭapa in a typical temple of simple design.

Fig. 3. Nāgara, drāviḍa and vesara types.

Fig. 4. Details of a śikhara (Orissa type)

Fig. 5. Plan and elevation of a temple based on a maṇḍala.

Fig. 6. Vāstupuruṣa.

6A. Coronary section through a pratiṣtha showing Ṣaḍādhāra pratiṣṭha.

Fig. 7. A typical icon in standing posture with mudrā.

Fig. 8. Tālamāna system with the measurement of the palm and the face as a fundamental unit.

Fig. 9. A typical ratha (temple car used for processions.)

Fig. 10. Dhvajastaṁbha.

Fig. 11. Balipīṭha.

Fig. 12. Dīpastaṁbha.

BIBLIOGRAPHY

1. ACHARYA (Prasanna Kumar), A Dictionary of Hindu Architecture, treating of Sanskrit Architectural terms, with illustrative quotations from śilpaśāstras, General literature and Archaeological records. (Varanasi, Bharatiya Publishing House, 1979)

2. BANERJEA (Jitendra Nath), The Development of Hindu Iconography, Edn. 2,revised and enlarged, (Calcutta, University of Calcutta,1956)

3. KRAMRISCH (Stella), The Hindu Temple, Vols.I and II (Delhi,Motilal Banarsidas,1976)

4. KRISHNARAO (A.N.) Ed., Bharatiya Samskriti Darsahna (in Kannada) Bangalore, Govt.of Karnataka, (Dept.of Literature and Cultural Development.1962)

5. MICHELL (George), The Hindu Temple: An Introduction to its Meaning and Forms (London,Paul Elek,1977)

6. SHUKLA (Lalit Kumar), A study of Hindu Art and Architecture with special reference to Terminology (Varanasi, Chowkhamba Sanskrit Series Office, 1972)

7. SRINIVASA AYYANGAR(A), and SRINIVASA AYYANGAR (T), Bharatakhandada Dėvalayagalu (in Kannada) Vol.I (Mysore,1978)

8. SRINIVASAN (K.R.), Temples of South India, Edn.2 revised (New Delhi, National Book Trust,1979)

9. STUTLEY (Margaret and James), A Dictionary of Hinduism, its Mythology, Folklore and Development 1500 B.C.-A.D.1500 (Bombay, Allied Publishers,1977)

1
Introduction

History of mankind has shown that man cannot live without God. 'If God did not exist, it would be necessary to invent him!' declared Voltaire. Belief in God, in a cosmic Power or cosmic Law, in a superhuman Spirit or Being is basic to all cultures. It is as it were, in the very blood of mankind. Once this fact is recognised, it becomes irrelevant whether this belief has been brought about by man's awe, wonder and fear of the powers of nature, or by the teachings of god-men who are supposed to have had mystical experiences of that God.

Man is human and not divine! This is so, atleast, as long as he is conscious of his frailties and impulses. It is exactly because of this that he turns towards the Divine in times of need. Though the Divine transcends all temporal limitations, man the human, needs a temporal set-up that can help him to visualise the Divine or establish contact with it. This is precisely where a symbol or an image or a place of worship comes to his rescue.

All religions have their sacred places, places of worship. All words which denote such places of worship, etymologically speaking, mean more or less, the same thing. 'Devālaya' means a 'house of God'. 'Temple' and 'Synagogue' mean a 'building for religious exercises' and a 'house for communal worship'. A 'Church' also means the same thing. A 'Masjid' is a 'place of prostration before God'.

2
A Brief History of Hindu Temples

How and when the first temple took its birth is anybody's guess. Temples do not seem to have existed during the Vedic age. The practice of preparing images of the deities mentioned in the Vedic mantras might have come into vogue by the end of the Vedic period. The view that the yāgaśālā of the Vedic period gradually got metamorphosed into temples by the epic period owing to the influence of the cults of devotion is widely accepted.

The earliest temples were built with perishable materials like timber and clay. Cave-temples, temples carved out of stone or built with bricks came later. Heavy stone structures with ornate architecture and sculpture belong to a still later period.

Considering the vast size of this country, it is remarkable that the building of temples has progressed more or less on a set pattern. This is because there is a basic philosophy behind the temple, its meaning and significance, which will be explained later.

In spite of the basic pattern being the same, varieties did appear, gradually leading to the evolution of different styles in temple architecture. Broadly speaking, these can be bifurcated into the northern and the southern styles. The northern style, technically called nāgara, is distinguished by the curvilinear towers. The southern style, known as the drāviḍa, has its towers in the form of truncated pyramids. A third style, vesara by name, is sometimes added, which combines in itself both these styles (Fig3).

The earliest temples in north and central India which have withstood the vagaries of time belong to the Gupta period, 320-650 A.D. Mention may be made of the temples at Sanchi, Tigawa (near Jabbalpur in Madhya Pradesh), Bhumara (in Madhya Pradesh), Nachna (Rajasthan) and Deogarh (near Jhansi, Uttar Pradesh).

Among the earliest surviving temples in South India are those found in Tamil Nadu and northern Karnataka. The cradle of Draviḍan school of architecture was the Tamil country which evolved from the earliest Buddhist shrines which were both rock-cut and structural. The later rock-cut temples which belong roughly to the period 500-800 A.D.were mostly Brāhmanical or Jain, patronised by three great ruling dynasties of the south, namely the Pallavas of Kāñchī in the east, the Cālukyas of Bādāmi in the west and the Pāṇḍyas of Madurai in the far south. With the decline of the Cālukyas of Bādāmi in the 8th century A.D, the Rāṣṭrakūṭas of Malkhed came to power and they made great contributions to the development of south Indian temple architecture. The Kailāsanātha temple at Ellora belongs to this period.

In the west (northern Karnataka) the Aihoḷe and Paṭṭadakal group of temples (5th to 7th centuries) show early attempts to evolve an acceptable regional style based on tradition. Among the better known early structural temples at Aihoḷe are the Huchimalliguḍi and Durgā temples as also the Lāḍkhān temple, all assigned to the period 450-650 A.D. Equally important are the temples of Kāśīnātha, Pāpanātha, Saṅgameśvara,

Virūpākṣa and others in Paṭṭadakal near Aihoḷe as also the Svargabrahmā temple at Ālampur (Andhra Pradesh). It is in some of these temples, built by the later Cālukyas, that we come across the vesara style, a combination of the northern and the southern modes.

There are many ancient texts laying down the formal architectural styles prevalent in the various regions so that the comprehensive text called the Vāstu Śāstra has its sources in the Sūtras, Purāṇas and Āgamas besides Tāntric literature and the Bṛhat Saṁhitā. But all of them are agreed that basically styles can be divided into nāgara, drāviḍa and vesara. They employ respectively the square, octagon and the apse or circle in their plan. In its later evolution when the vesara style adopted the square for the sanctum, the circular or stellar plan was retained for the vimāna. These three styles do not pertain strictly to three different regions but as indicating only the temple groups. The vesara, for instance, which came to prevail mostly in western Deccan and south Karnataka was a derivation from the apsidal chapels of the early Buddhist period which the Brāhmanical faith adopted and vastly improved. In its origin, the vesara is as much north Indian as it is west Deccanese. Similarly among the 6th-7th century shrines of Aihoḷe and Paṭṭadakal we find evidance of nāgara style in the prāsādas or vimānas. The drāviḍa or Tamilian style became very popular throughout south India only from the Vijayanagar times onward. While the prāsāda or vimāna of the nāgara style rises vertically from its base in a curvilinear form, that of the drāviḍa rises like a stepped pyramid, tier upon tier. The northern style came to prevail in Rajasthan Upper India, Orissa, the Vindhyan uplands and Gujarat.

During the next thousand years (from 600 to 1600 A.D.) there was a phenomenal growth in temple architecture both in quantity and quality. The first in the series of southern or drāviḍian architecture was initiated by the Pallavas(600-900 A.D.). The rock-cut temples at Mahābalipuram (of the 'ratha'type) and the structural temples like the shore temple at Mahābalipuram and the Kailāsanātha and Vaikuṇṭha Perumāḷ temples in Kancheepuram (700-800 A.D.) are the best representatives of the Pallava style. The Pallavas laid the foundations of the draviḍian school which blossomed to its full extent during the Coḷas,the Pāṇḍyas, the Vijayanagar kings and the Nāyaks. The temples, now built of stone, became bigger, more complex and ornate with sculptures. Draviḍian architecture reached its glory during the

Coḷa period (900-1200 A.D.) by becoming more imposing in size and endowed with happy proportions. Among the most beautiful of the Coḷa temples is the Bṛhadīśvara temple at Tanjore with its 66 metre high vimāna,the tallest of its kind. The later Pāṇḍyans who succeeded the Coḷas improved on the Coḷas by introducing elaborate ornamentation and big sculptural images, many-pillared halls, new annexes to the shrine and towers(gopurams) on the gateways. The mighty temple complexes of Madurai and Srirangam in Tamil Nadu set a pattern for the Vijayanagar builders (1350-1565 A.D.) who followed the draviḍian tradition. The Pampāpati and Viṭṭhala temples in Hampi are standing examples of this period. The Nāyaks of Madurai who succeeded the Vijayanagar kings (1600 to 1750 A.D.) made the draviḍian temple complex even more elaborate by making the gopurams very tall and ornate and adding pillared corridors within the temple long compound.

Contemporaneous with the Coḷas (1100-1300 A.D.),the Hoysaḷas who ruled the Kannada country improved on the Cālukyan style by building extremely ornate temples in many parts of Karnataka noted for the sculptures in the walls, depressed ceilings, lathe-turned pillars and fully sculptured vimānas. Among the most famous of these temples are the ones at Belur, Halebid and Somanāthapura in south Karnataka, which are classified under the vesara style.

In the north, the chief developments in Hindu temple architecture took place in Orissa (750-1250 A.D.) and Central India (950-1050 A.D.) as also Rajasthan (10th and 11th Century A.D.) and Gujarat (11th-13th Century A.D.). The temples of Liṅgarājā (Bhubaneshwar), Jagannātha (Puri) and Sūrya (Konarak) represent the Orissan style. The temples at Khajurāho built by the Chandellas, the Sūrya temple at Modhera (Gujarat) and other temples at Mt.Abu built by the Solaṅkis have their own distinct features in Central Indian architecture. Bengal with its temples built in bricks and terracotta tiles and Kerala with its temples having peculiar roof structure suited to the heavy rainfall of the region, developed their own localised special styles.

Mention may also be made here of the various Hindu temples outside India, especially in the South East Asian countries. The earliest of such Hindu temples are found in Java; for instance, the Siva temples at Dieng and (idong Songo built by the kings of Śailendra dynasty (8th-9th century A.D.).

The group of temples of Lara Jonggrang at Pranbanan (9th or 10th century A.D.), is a magnificent example of Hindu temple architecture. Other temples worth mentioning are: the temple complex at Panataran (java) built by the kings of Majapahit dynasty (14th century A.D.), the rock-cut temple facades at Tampaksiring of Bali (11th century A.D.),the 'mother' temple at Besakh of Bali (14th century A.D.),the Chen La temples at Sambor Prei Kuk in Cambodia (7th-8th century A.D.)., the temple of Banteay Srei at Angkor (10th century A.D.) and the celebrated Angkor Vat complex (12th century A.D.) built by Sūrya Varman II.

3
Symbology of the Temple

The temple is a link between man and God, between the earthly life and the divine life, between the actual and the ideal. As such it has got to be symbolic.

The word 'devālaya' which is frequently used to denote at temple, actually means 'the house of

God'. It is the place where God dwells on earth to bless mankind. It is His house, His palace. Infact, there is another word to denote a temple,'Prāsāda', which means a palace with a very pleasing appearance. When looked at this way, the dhvajastaṁbha represents the flagpost on which flies the insignia of the deity. The outer walls, prākāra, are the walls of the fort. The gopuram (high tower at the entrance) is the main gateway.

'Vimāna' is another word which is often used to denote a temple in general, and the garbhagṛha *(sanctum sanctorum)* in particular. The simple etymological meaning is a 'well-proportioned structure'. As an extension of this meaning derived from the root-verb mā (=to measure), it signifies God the Creator, as a combination of Śiva and Śakti, who 'measures out' as it were, this limited universe from out of Himself, the unlimited principle. It further means an aeroplane. It is the aeroplane of the gods landed on the earth to bless mankind.

Pilgrimage has an important place in the Hindu religion. A place of pilgrimage is called a tīrtha(=means) and is invariably associated with a temple. Hence the temple is called a tīrtha. The temple helps us as a means of crossing the ocean of saṁsāra (transmigratory existence).

Even more significant is the conception that its plan and elevation. Horizontally the garbhagṛha represents the head and the gopuram the feet of the deity. Other parts of the building complex are identified with other parts of the body. For instance, the śukanāsī (also spelled as sukhanāsi or sukanāsī) or ardhamaṇṭapa (the small enclosure in front of the garbhagṛha) is the nose; the antarāla[1] (the passage next to the previous one, leading to passage next to the previous one, leading to the main maṇṭapa called nṛttamaṇṭapa) is the neck; the various maṇṭapas are the body; the prākāras (surrounding walls) are the hands and so on. Vertically, the garbhagṛha represents the neck, the śikhara(superstructure over the garbhagṛha) the head, the kalaśa (finial) the tuft of hair (śikhā) and so on.

The temple also represents God in a cosmic form, with the various worlds located on different parts of His body. The bhūloka (earth) forms His

---

[1] In many temples the antarāla is merged with the śukanāsī itself and not built separately.

feet and Satyaloka (also called Brahmaloka) forms His śikhā, with the other lokas (bhuvarloka, svarloka, maharloka, janaloka and tapoloka) forming the appropriate parts of His body. The ground, represents bhūloka. The adhiṣṭhānapīṭha (the base-slab below the image), the staṁbhas (pillars), prastara (entablature, supported above the pillars), śikhara (superstructure over the garbhagṛha), āmalasāra (lower part of the final) and the stūpikā (topknot or the finial) represent respectively the worlds bhuvaḥ, svaḥ, mahaḥ, janaḥ, tapaḥ, and satyam.

The temple also represents the Meruparvata the mythical golden mountain described in the purāṇas (Hindu mythological literature), as the centrai point of the universe,round which (in all directions) are spread the various worlds?

Again, the temple represents this world in all its aspects, the actual and the ideal. The imposing gopurams at the entrance reflect the awesome grandeur of the external world. The friezes and the sculptures on the external walls of the temple proper, depict the animal world and the mundane life of the ordinary human beings including the ridiculous side and the aberrations.[2] These are followed by the scenes from the epic and mythological literature as also religious symbols and icons of gods and goddesses, to remind the onlookers of our great cultural and religious heritage.

If the temple symbolises the body of God on the macrocosmic plane, it equally symbolises the body of man on the microcosmic plane. The names of the various parts of the temple are the very names used to denote the various parts of human body! Look at the following technical names: pādukā, pāda, caraṇa, aṅghri, jaṅghā, ūru, gala, grīva, kaṇṭha, śira, śīrṣa, karṇa, nāsika, śikhā. Pāda (foot) is the column, Jaṅghā (shank) is part of the superstructure over the base. Gala or grīva (neck) is the part

---

[2] Criticism is often voiced against the mithuna figures (figures of amorous couples) that adorn most of the temples on their exterior walls. These figures, obviously connected with fertility rites, are considered to be auspicious. More often, they are iconographical representations of creation and of the bipolar nature of this created world, which is described in philosophical treatises as arising out of the union of prakṛti and puruṣa (nature and spirit). Uninhibited eroticism as found in the temples at Konarak (Orissa) and Khajuraho (Madhya Pradesh) is perhaps the outcome of Tāntricism.

between mouldings which resembles the neck. Nāsikā (nose) is any noseshaped architectural part and so on. The garbhagṛha represents the heart and the image,the antaryamin (the indwelling Lord). This symbology tries to impress upon us the need to seek the Lord within our heart and not outside.

The temple also represents the subtle body with the seven psychic centres or cakras. The garbhagṛha represents the anāhata cakra (the fourth psychic centre in the region of the heart) and the topmost part of the kalaśa point to the sahasrāra (seventh and the last centre situated at the top of the head). The first three centres (mūlādhāra, svādhiṣṭhāna and maṇipūra situated respectively near the anus, sex-organ and navel) are below the ground level. The fifth and the sixth (viśuddha and ājñā cakras, situated at the root of the throat and in between the eyebrows) are on the śikhara area.

Very often , the ground-plan of a temple is a maṇḍala (Fig.5). Hence whatever interpretation is given to a maṇḍala can also be extended to the temple itself. A maṇḍala is a geometric diagram with occult potentialities. Symmetry is its chief characteristic. The created world which is the perfect handicraft of a perfect Creator, can best be represented by a symmetrical and well-proportioned maṇḍala. The movement in the maṇḍala, as far as the devotee is concerned, is from the outer details to the inner centre, which is a point. The point represents the one creative Principle,the Deity, from which everything has evolved. The devotee has to start from outside, pass through circuitous routes and successive stages to come to the centre. Similarly the devotee who enters the temple has to pass through several gates, courtyards and passages, leaving the grand externals, and progress towards the garbhagṛha, the very heart of the temple complex, housing the one cosmic Principle.

4

Construction of a Temple Typical Steps

Building of temples is considered to be an extremely pious act, bringing great religious merit. Hence kings and rich people were eager to spend their wealth on it. All the various steps involved in it were performed either as religious rites or with religious overtones.

Let us now try to describe the typical steps commonly involved in building a temple. The yajamāna (lit. the sacrificer; here, the financier and builder) must first choose a proper guide or sthāpaka or ācārya for overall guidance and supervision. This ācārya must be a pious brāhmaṇa, with a sinless life. He must be an expert in art, architecture and rituals. The ācārya then chooses the sthapati (chief architect) and puts him in charge of the whole construction. The sthapati commands a status and respect equal to that of the ācārya. He is assisted by the sūtragrāhin (surveyor),the takṣaka (sculptor) and the vardhakin (builder, plasterer and painter).

From the day of saṅkalpa (religious resolve), the yajamāna and the ācārya have to take certain religious vows and lead a very strict life in accordance with those vows.

The first and foremost step in the building of a temple is the selection of a suitable site situated in or near a holy place and endowed with natural beauty and peace. The site has then to be cleared of all its vegetation. Evil spirits have to be exorcised and the place purified.

Assuming that the detailed designs and engineering drawings have already been prepared, the next item is vāstuvinyāsa, drawing the vāstumaṇḍala on the site of the temple construction at an appropriate auspicious time. The cosmic man embodying the whole creation including the different deities of the Hindu pantheon in the different limbs and parts of his body, is technically called the vāstupuruṣa (Fig.6). The maṇḍala is a geometrical drawing of 64 squares which represents him. Once the vāstumaṇḍala is drawn ceremonially, it becomes 'alive', with the vāstupuruṣa fixed on it. Later, the image or the symbol of the deity will have to be installed in the centre of this maṇḍala at the appropriate time.

Another important religious ceremony connected with the various stages of construction is aṅkurārpaṇa (rite of the seeds and their germination). Its main purpose is to facilitate the fruition of the work without obstructions and obstacles. It is performed before the construction starts, before laying the last brick or stone (mūrdheṣṭakā) into superstructure, prior to the installation of the main image, before the, opening of the eyes' (akṣimocana) of the image and so on. The rite consists of placing the seeds of different varieties of rice, sesamum, mustard etc., in 16 copper vessels in front of Soma (the lord of germination) and offering them to the concerned deity after germination

Next comes silānyāsa or foundation stone laying ceremony. It is the laying of the first stone (square in shape) or brick signifying the start of construction. It is laid in the north-western corner of the building plan,drawn on the ground after excavating the foundation to the required depth. After this, the construction of the foundation is taken up.

The foundation is built and the ground filled up,up to the plinth level, except in the middle portion of the garbhagṛha which is filled up to three-fourths only. In the centre of this place, the ādhāraśilā (a base stone) is placed, over which are deposited the following articles in that order: a pot (called nidhikuṁbha), a tortoise and a lotus, all made of stone; a tortoise and a lotus made of silver; a tortoise and a lotus made of gold. From there, a funnel-shaped tube called yoganālā,made of copper leads upto the plinth. The whole thing is covered by another stone slab called brahmaśilā. Later on, the image of the deity is established over this (Fig.6A)

Another extremely important rite which is performed during temple construction is the garbhanyāsa ("insemination" of the temple site). A casket or tray of copper, whose dimensions are proportional to the dimensions of the temple, is ceremonially lowered into the ground on an auspicious night after filling its 25 squares with various articles and duly worshipping it. It represents the Mother Earth and the ceremony itself is done with a view to achieving the smooth consummation of the temple project.

Materials used for construction like stones, bricks and wood should be procured newly from their sources, for which also there are guidelines. All the tools and implements used in the construction should be worshipped.

After the foundation is built up to the basement level, the superstructure is built either with pillars or with walls or a combination of both. Doors, openings, niches, windows and porches with suitable decorations are added at the appropriate stages, ending finally with the śikhara (the crest or the finial) (Fig.4).

The most important part of temple construction is the preparation and installation of the image of the main deity as also the images of the subsidiary deities.

5
Essential Parts of A Typical Temple [3]

The most important part of a temple, its very heart as it were, is the garbhagṛha or *sanctum sanctorum*. This is usually square with a low roof and with no doors or windows except for the front opening. The image of the deity is stationed in the geometrical centre. The whole place is completely dark, except for the light that comes through the front opening. Over the roof of the whole shrine is a small tower. This towerִ is quite high in the North Indian temples and of low or medium height in the South Indian temples

In some temples, a pradakṣiṇapatha (a circumambulatory passage) is provided just round the garbhagṛha, to enable the devotees to go round the deity. Only vesara temples do not have this passage.

In front of the garbhagṛha and contiguous to it is the mukhamaṇṭapa, sometimes called sukanāsī or ardhamaṇṭapa, depending upon its proportion relative to that of the garbhagṛha. Apart from being used as a passage , it is also used to keep the articles

[3] See Fig. 1 and Fig. 2.

of worship including naivedya (food offerings) on special occasions.

Then comes antarāla, a narrow passage connecting the garbhagr̄ha and the mukhamaṇṭapa to the maṇṭapa (pavilion or hall). As already stated, in most of the temples the antarāla is identical with the mukhamantapa or śukanāsī.

The maṇṭapa (also called nṛttamaṇṭapa or navaraṅga) is a big hall and is used for congregational religious acts like singing, dancing, recitation of mythological texts, religious discourses and so on.

The dhvajastaṁbha (flagpost) [Fig. 10] in front of either the garbhagṛha or antarāla or the maṇṭapa is another common feature. It represents the flagpost of the 'King of kings. The lāñchana (insignia) made of copper or brass fixed like a flag to the top of the post varies according to the deity in the temple. The figure on the lāñchana is invariably that of the vāhana (carrier vehicle) of the deity. For instance, in Siva temples it contains Nandi. In Devi temples it is the lion that finds its place. In Viṣṇu temples Garuḍa gets that honour.

The balipīṭha (pedestal of sacrificial offerings) [Fig. 11] with a lotus or the footprints of the deity is fixed near the dhvajastaṁbha, but nearer to the deity. Red-coloured offerings like rice mixed with vermillion powder, are kept on this at appropriate stages during the performance of rituals. This indicates the feeding of the parivāradevatās (attendant and associate deities).

There is every reason to believe that the yūpastaṁbha (Sacrificial post) and the balipiṭha (sacrificial pedestal) of the Vedic age have become metamorphosed into the dhvajastaṁbha and the balipīṭha.

The whole temple is surrounded by a high wall (prākāra) with one main and three subsidiary gates, opening in the cardinal directions. A gopuram (high tower, sometimes called as the Cow-gate) adorns these gateways.

Inside the prākāra, three will be minor temples or shrines for the minor deities, connected with the main deity. For instance, in a Śiva temple, the minor shrines are dedicated to Gaṇapati, Pārvatī, Subrahmaṇya and Caṇḍeśvara. In a Viṣṇu temple, Lakṣmī, Hanumān and Garuḍa find a place. In a Durgā temple, Siva, Gaṇapati and subrahmaṇya will be found.

Apart from these, the temple precincts include a yāgaśālā, (sacrificial shed), pākaśālā (cooking shed) and kitchen, place for the utsavamūrti (processional image carried during the car festivals), well or a puskariṇī (tank), flower garden, stores and other essential structures connected with the management of the temple as also the rituals.

A dīpastaṁbha (lamp post) [Fig. 12] is another constituent of a temple complex often found in South Indian temples. It is situated either in front of the balipīṭha or outside the main gate. The top of this post has a budshaped chamber to receive the lamp.

6
Iconography

Since the whole temple is built to house the image of the deity, a few words about Indian iconography (science of preparing the images) will not be out of place here.

Indian iconography is a very ancient science and art. There are clear references to images in the Ṛgveda and to temples in the Atharvaveda. Subsequent ancient works contain innumerable references to the same.

Broadly speaking, the images in the Hindu temples fall into three groups: Śaiva, Śākta and Vaiṣṇava, respectively belonging to the three cults of Śiva, Śakti and Viṣṇu. The images, again, can be acala or dhruvabera (immovable) or cala (movable). The former are usually made of stone and are permanently fixed. The latter are usually made of metals like bronze or pañcaloha (alloy of five metals) and are used for taking out in procession on festive occasions,for bathing, for ritualistic worship etc. Sometimes, a third category, calācala (both movable and immovable) is added. When the same image that is kept and worshipped in the garbhagṛha is also taken out on the ratha (temple car)-as for instance in the case of the temple of Lord Jagannātha at Purī (Orissa)—it is called calācala.

Again, the images can be in three postures: sthānaka (standing) [Fig.7], āsana (sitting) and śayana (lying down). Only images of Viṣṇu are to be seen in the śayana posture also.

The particular aspects of the deities represented by the images can be recognised by seeing the mudrā (position of the hands and fingers), āsana (posture of legs and feet), cihna (symbol), vasana (dress) and ābharaṇa (ornaments). Among the mudrās and āsanas, abhayamudrā (assuring protection), varadamudrā (granting boons), padmāsana (lotus posture) and yogāsana (meditation posture) are most common. Śaiva and Śākta images have ḍamaru (drum), triśūla (trident), pāśa (noose), aṅkuśa (goad), bāṇa (arrow), khaḍga (sword) and so on, as their symbols. Cakra (discus), śaṅkha (conch), gadā (mace) and padma (lotus) are more common for Vaiṣṇava images. As regards dress and ornaments, they are too numerous to mention.

There are elaborate rules guiding the sculpturing of images. The height or length, width, girth as also the proportions of the various limbs—each one of these is fixed according to the tāla māna system. A 'tāla' is the measurement of the palm of hand (from the tip of the middle finger to the wrist) and is equal to the length of the face. The navatāla system wherein the total length or height of the image is nine times (nava=nine) the length of the face, is recommended for the images of gods.

In spite of all these rules and regulations the sculptor had freedom to show his skill. A beautiful face with the expression of the appropriate rasa (emotion or sentiment) was commended and recommended.

7
Religious Rites and Ceremonies

(a) Consecration Ceremony (partiṣṭhāvidhi):

Once the construction of a new temple is successfully completed, it is to be formally consecrated with appropriate rites and ceremonies. A separate pandal is erected in the north-eastern corner of the main structure wherein are performed all the important religious ceremonies.

Since the consecration is a very elaborate religious ceremony, only the most important steps will be described. After the usual pūjā and homa for the vāstupuruṣa, nine balis (offerings) are given to the minor (and usually fierce) deities, by placing the balis all round the temple and the deities are then requested to leave the place permanently. Then the ācārya, the yajamāna and their assistants enter the yāgaśālā and establish kalaśas (ceremonial pots filled with water, the number being up to a maximum of 32) all round the place. After certain preliminary rites, homas are performed in the several homakuṇḍas (1 or 5 or 9) to propitiate the main deity of the temple and other associated deities.

Meanwhile, the image of the main deity, after the ceremonial opening of its eyes (netronmīlana) will have been taken in the ratha (temple car) to a nearby source of water like a river or a pond and immersed in it for the first of the three adhivāsa ceremonies (adhivāsa=abode), called jalādhivāsa. From there, after three days, the image is brought in the ratha to the yāgaśālā and then put in grains for another three days (dhānyādhivāsa). It is then taken out and put on a specially prepared bed for three days more (śayyādhivāsa).

In the centre of the garbhagṛha, a yantra (a gold plate with occult designs), some precious stones and minerals as also some seeds are placed.

Then comes aṣṭabandha. Eight materials like conch, whitestone, lac, perfume etc., are powdered nicely and mixed with butter or oil to form a paste which is then put on the yantra and other materials mentioned previously. Over this the image is fixed. This image is then connected by a gold wire or a long thread, to the main homakuṇḍa in the yāgaśālā. This is called nāḍīsandhāna whereby the nāḍis or internal passages will become opened up as it were, to receive life. The deity is then invoked into the image by prāṇapratiṣṭhā (a simple ceremony for infusing life-force) and a simple worship is performed.

The main kalaśa from the yāgaśālā is then brought and the image bathed with that water. This is called kuṁbhābhiṣeka. This is then followed by elaborate worship, offerings and waving of lights.

The ācārya, the yajamāna, the sthapati and their assistants will then take a ceremonial bath (called avabhṛtha-snāna) indicating thereby that they have successfully completed a great and meritorious act.

(a) Devotees and poor people of the place are then sumptuously fed.

(b) Daily Worship (nityapūjā):

Once a temple is built and ceremonially consecrated, daily worship must be done regularly. This daily worship can be done from a minimum of once, up to a maximum of six times (before sunrise, after sunrise, between 8 and 9 a.m., noon, evening and night). During each worship, all the dress and ornaments of the deity should be removed and the image should be bathed successively with oil, ghee, milk, water and scented water. It should then be dressed again, smeared with sandal paste and decorated with ornaments.

Food articles should then be offered. All these are done after closing the doors of the garbhagṛha. After opening the doors, waving of lights and several upacāras (items of special service) are done, including chanting of hymns and music.

Ceremonial worship is also done to the consort of the main deity and minor deities associated with it.

(c) Occasional Worship (naimittika-pūjā):

Worship done on special occasions like Śivarātri, Vaikuṇṭha Ekādaśī or Dasara is called naimittika-pūjā. This worship differs from place to place, or even from temple to temple. It is done in addition to the daily worship. Special homa, japa (repitition of the divine name), abhiṣeka (bathing the image) and elaborate worship are its distinctive features. The utsavamūrti, meant to be taken out in procession, will be well-decorated and exhibited to the devotees.

(d) Rathotsava and Brahmotsava:

On the special occasions mentioned above, religious celebrations may be spread over a number of days. The biggest festival among these is called Brahmotsava (Brahma=big). This is also called rathotsava since the utsavamūrti is taken out in a procession in the temple car. Beating the drum (bherītāḍana), hoisting the flag of the deity (dhvajārohaṇa), inviting the deity to the yāgaśālā (āvāhana), establishing the kalaśas and performing homa are some of the more important aspects of the festival. The temple car is taken out two days before the close of the festival. In some temples where there are facilities of a river or a big tank, teppotsava (boat-festival) is also performed on the next day of the rathotsava.

Rathas (Fig.9) being the replicas of temples. Rathotsavas are very popular. The whole ratha and the deity are elegantly decorated and the procession with its music, lights, crackers and entertainment becomes very attractive . Hundreds of devotees without any distinction of caste, creed or colour draw the car, shoulder to shoulder. Devotees unable to go to the temple due to any reason, can have the darśan on their doorsteps and can even offer their private worship.

8
Temple Arts and Crafts

Kings, as lords and masters of the country over which they rule, are well-known for their encouragement to arts, crafts and artisans. The temple which houses the King of kings, should not lag behind! That is why we find the temples, especially the bigger ones, acting as the biggest employers and providing the greatest security and encouragement to the artisans and artists. Apart from sculpturing stone images or casting metalic ones, the other arts and crafts associated with the temples can be listed as follows: music, dance, preparation of musical instruments, embriodery work on cloth, tailoring, preparation of perfumes and scents, making of flower-garlands, cooking of special dishes, astrology, building the ratha, etching or embossing on metal plates used in various ways, making of lamp-posts and stands, as also pūjā vessels in brass, bronze and copper, painting, gold and silver smithy, ivorycraft and so on. Development of these crafts and their flourishing trade over centuries are largely due to the temples.

9
The Temple and the Devotee

When we want to meet our superiors or persons highly placed in life, we observe certain etiquette, norms and decorum. Therefore it is but natural that the devotee who wants to visit the Lord of the universe in a temple, is expected to observe a certain code of conduct. Taking bath, wearing freshly washed clothes is a must. If and when possible, this should be done in the Puṣkariṇī attached to the temple. After entering the precincts of the temple, he should observe silence and try to withdraw the mind into the thoughts of God. After having the darśan of the deity and getting his individual worship if any, performed, he should circumambulate the main shrine three, five or seven times. Then he should bow down to the deity from a place outside the dhvajastambha, taking care to see that his feet do not point in the direction of any of the minor deities. Visiting the shrines of the minor deities is his next duty. Before leaving the precincts of the temple, he should sit quietly in some corner and meditate. Since distribution of alms to deserving beggars in the vicinity of the temple is considered meritorious, the devotees are advised to do so.

Apart from these general rules to be observed by the devotee, he should also be aware of the daivāpacāras, modes of behaviour which will offend the deity in the temple. This is very important because when a temple is built and the image consecrated ceremonially, the power of the deity will manifest itself through that image. This is technically called arcāvatāra.

The following are some of the modes of behaviour which will offend the deity in the temple, and bring misery and suffering upon the transgressor: not observing the rules concerning personal, environmental and ceremonial cleanliness, missing the important festivals of the temple, not making obeisance or circumambulation, carelessly treating the things offered to the deity, not offering the best kind of things even though one can afford to do so, disposing of the offered articles to people who have no faith or devotion, engaging in purely secular and nonreligious activities in the presence of the deity, boisterious behaviour, observing caste restrictions, misusing the things belonging to the temple and so son.

10
The Temple and the Priest

It will not be out of place to discuss here the role of the priest in a Hindu temple. Since it is the chief responsibility of the head-priest and his assistants to maintain the spiritual atmosphere of the temple, a strict code of conduct is enjoined upon them. They are expected to lead a very strict and pure life. They should know all the rituals and ceremonies connected with the temple worship and festivities. They should observe all the rules concerning personal and ceremonial purity. They should perform the worship with śraddhā (faith) and devotion. They should not misuse the temple property in any way. On the other hand they should protect it. They should have genuine concern for the devotees and should treat them with sympathy and understanding. Broadmindedness and a liberal outlook should be an additional qualification for modern priests.

11
The Temple and the Society

Throughout our history, the temple has exercised an enormous influence on our social life. Apart from keeping the torch of dharma urning aloft, the temple has been a great cementing factor. Its shrine and icons have given peace to the frustrated minds. The construction and maintenance of the building have provided employment to the architects, artisans, sculptors and labourers. Religious discourses and musical discourses (pravacanas and harikathās) have helped the propagation of religion, Music, dance and other fine arts have received great encouragement and provided pure and elevating type of entertainment to the devotees. Being a centre of learning, the temple helped in the acquisition and propagation of knowledge. Both scholars and students found shelter there. With its enormous wealth, it also acted as a bank to the needy, giving easy credits. The granaries of the temple helped to feed the hungry, and those unable to earn their livelihood due to disease and deformity. There are several instances of even hospitals and dispensaries being run by the temple. The temple often played the role of a court of law for settling disputes. The temple also gave shelter to the people during wars. Thus the temple was all-in-all in the social life of our country for centuries.

It may not be out of place if we describe here in a few words, the system of the temple-dancers, commonly known as devadāsīs. If the god in the temple is considered to be a living being, it is but natural that the devotees should deem it a privilege to offer him all enjoyments to which an emperor or a king is entitled and accustomed! The system of offering unmarried girls to the temple for the service of the deity might have originated this way. And, this is not peculiar to India alone. There is evidence to prove that in ancient Babylonia,

Cyprus, Greece, Mesapotamia, Egypt, Syria and Arabia, as also in the South East Asian countries such a system has existed.

This system was opposed by the brāhmaṇas. However, due to the pressure of the kings and noblemen it came to stay.

The girls chosen to become devadāsīs would be married to the deity in the temple in a ceremonial way. Their main duties consisted of cleaning the temple, fanning the image, carrying lights, singing and dancing before the deity and the devotees and so on.

The system might have started some time during the 3rd cent. A.D. It soon degenerated into prostitution, thanks to the notorious human weaknesses. The practice of the kings and the noblemen of entertaining their important guests with music and dancing by the slave girls and maids of their harem might have been extended to the devadāsīs also, so much so, that it drove them to prostitution in course of time.

But for some pockets in Andhra Pradesh, Karnataka, Maharashtra and Tamil Nadu, the system has almost disappeared.

12
Epilogue

Thus it is seen that the temple which represents God and His abode, creation and the Creator, man and his true Self, has played no insignificant part in the life of our society. If today its effect has waned considerably, it is worth making a study of the maladies affecting it and try to find out appropriate remedies.

The basic malady from which all other maladies spring is the lack of proper organisation. This again is the outcome of the fact that the Hindu society is the most disorganised society in the whole world! Though organisation and order are found in bits and pieces, here and there, in small and well-knit groups, the Hindu society as a whole suffers from an utter lack of discipline due to the absence of a central church controlling all sections of the Hindu society and claiming the loyalty of all. This problem is as urgent as it is big. It is high time that the highly respected and influential religious leaders of the Hindu society make an earnest attempt to tackle this problem on a war-footing. The earlier, the better. When the Hindus have enough catholicity to accept all the great religious system of the world as equally valid and true, they can certainly extend that catholicity towards their own innumerable sects and groups, thereby achieving greater amalgamation and cohesion!

In the scheme of restoration of the temples to their former glory and pride of place, the first problem that confront us is that of the many historical temples which are in dilapidated condition and wherein regular worship has been totally abandoned. Then there are temples where worship is still in vogue but which need renovation badly. The need to build new temples in the new townships and colonies coming up all over the country, especially in industrial project areas, cannot also be overemphasised. Hence the constitution of an All India Temple Trust to which not only devotees but also the richer temples in the country will contribute should seriously be considered. This should be an autonomous body and can release the funds to the concerned temple projects as and when necessary.

The second important problem is the one concerning the priests and other staff managing the temple. Efforts should be made to set up enough number of institutions to train up the priests properly on the lines of the āgamaśāstras. Only such trained personnel should be employed in the temples. Though simple living and high thinking should be a basic concept to be integrated with their training, they should be paid decent salaries so that they are not forced to develop the 'panda-psychology' which is now rampant and against which almost everybody is railing without understanding their problems and difficulties.

Apart from the spiritual atmosphere, even the physical atmosphere in the precincts of the temple is equally important, since the latter is conductive to the former. It is common knowledge that churches and mosques—even those situated in the socially and culturally backward areas—are kept clean and the votaries of these two religions (Christianity and Islam) maintain good discipline during their community prayers and worship. This is singularly lacking among the Hindus. This constitutes our third problem. Keeping the temples and the surrounding areas clean, maintaining discipline like following the queue system, observing silence at the time of worship and reasonable quietness at other times is a virtue that needs to be inculcated among our people. It is too much to expect the meagre temple staff to perform such tasks. The only way seems to be for the devotees living in the vicinity of the temple to form a volunteer crops of active men and women, including students, who should take turns to keep the temple area clean and educate the people visiting the temple. Hindu religious organisations can conduct short-term courses to train these volunteers. These volunteers will be an asset at the time of festivals and rathotsavas when they can perform other duties like taking care of the footwear, vehicles and personal belongings of the visiting devotees, regulating the queues, helping the aged and the infirm, distributing drinking water, giving emergency medical aid and so on.

Propagation of our religion among our people or, to put it succinctly, 'Hinduising the Hindus', is another problem, in the solution of which our temples can play an active role. Production of Hindu religious literature, written in nontechnical and popular language and at a cheap price is one of the effective methods of such propaganda. The volunteers can help in the sale of such literature. Organising regular classes on Hinduism both for children and for adults—the adults need it even more than the children!—is another activity that can be undertaken by the temples. Religious discourses, community bhajans, harikathas and staging of dramas which are in vogue even today, can be organised in more systematic ways.

It may be necessary to point out here one of the banes of our Hindu society: the tendency to convert cash into ornaments and ornamentation often superfluous, instead of spending the same on socially useful channels like increasing the facilities for the devotees and pilgrims visiting the temple, better emoluments to the temple staff, beautifying the area to create a better atmosphere and so on, apart from what has already been mentioned earlier.

The ignorance of the Hindus about their own religion is not only colossal but also ignominious. The temples, at least the bigger ones with larger incomes, can organise permanent exhibitions depicting the salient features of our religion and culture. The millions of devotees who visit these temples every year,can be educated at least in the fundamentals of our great religion[4].

Marriage is the most important sacrament in the life of a Hindu. The influence of Western culture is

---

[4] The bigger temples can also think of running educational, cultural and medical institutions to serve the public.

having a deleterious effect upon this. If marriages are compulsorily performed in the temple premises, or at least, solemnised by a suitable ritual in a temple, it may have greater stabilising effect. In addition, the Hindus should feel obliged to attend all the important festivals of a temple in their place should perform at least one important worship of their family in the temple.

The temple has occupied the most central place in the Hindu society for centuries and has been the greatest single factor in keeping it together. There is no reason why it should not be revitalised so that it can play even greater roles in the future. It is the sacred duty of all the leaders of the Hindu society to make every effort in this direction.

******

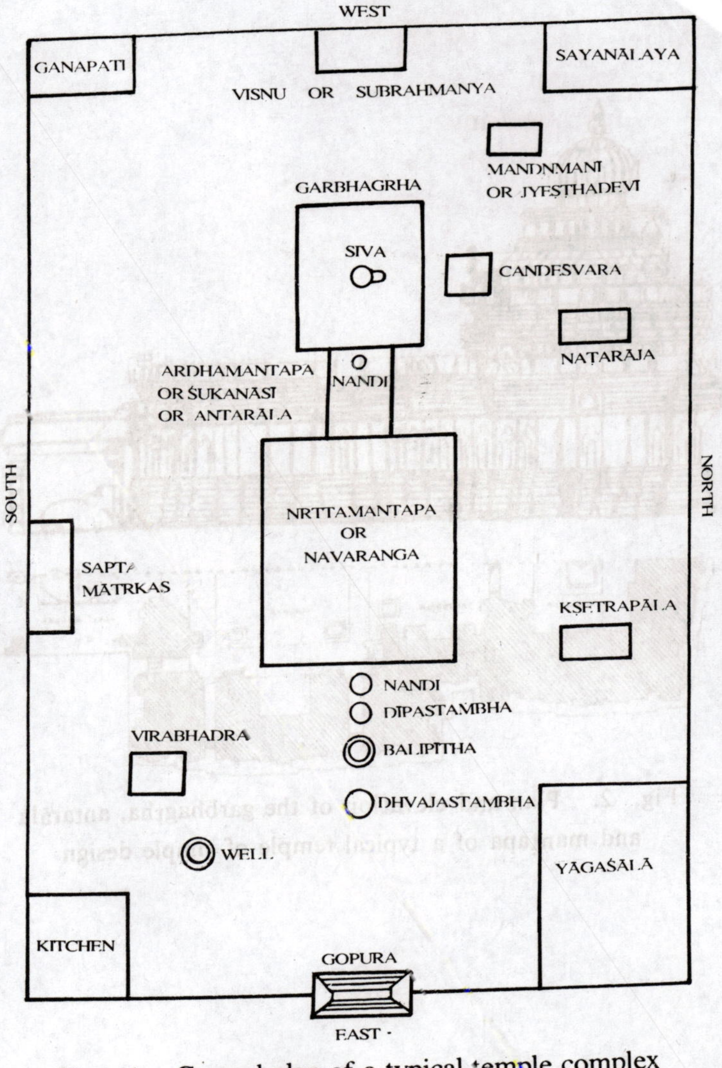

Fig. 1. Ground plan of a typical temple complex

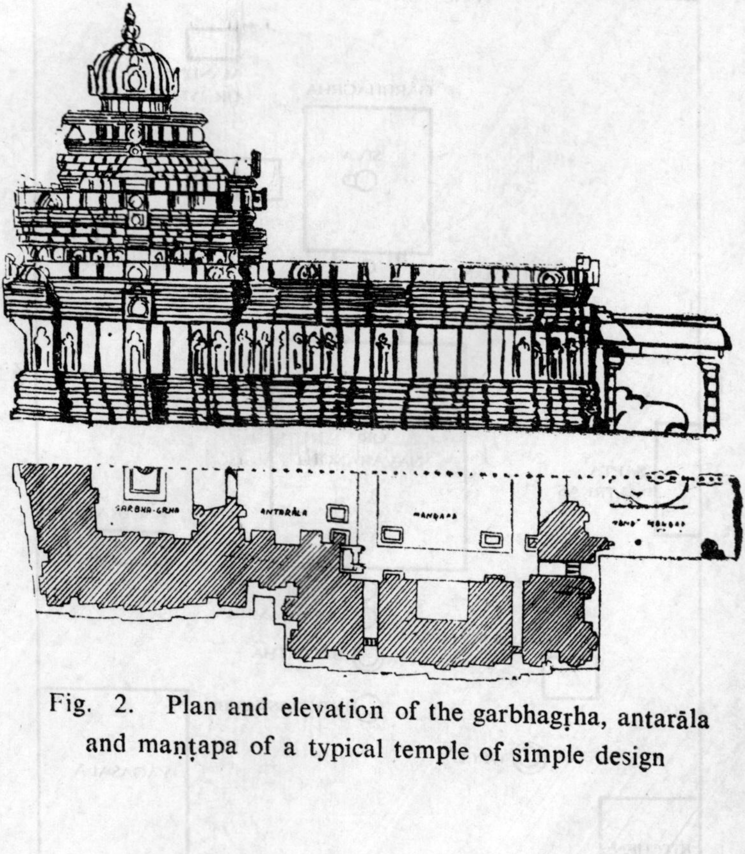

Fig. 2. Plan and elevation of the garbhagṛha, antarāla and maṇṭapa of a typical temple of simple design

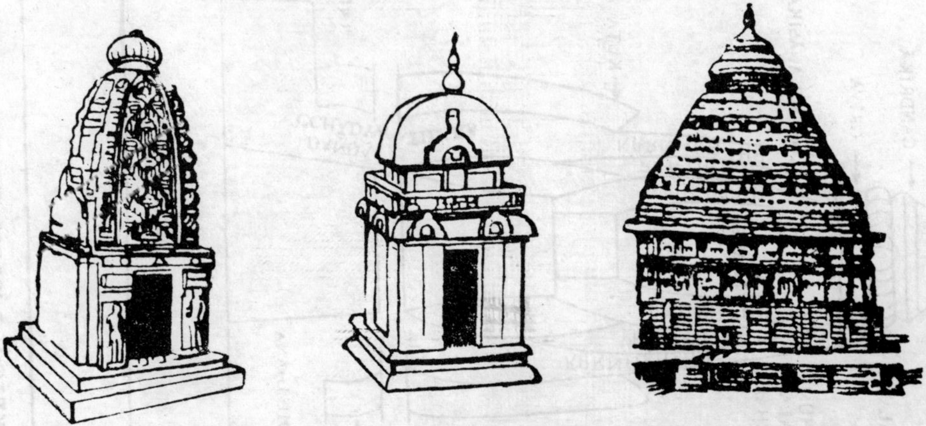

Fig. 3. Nāgara, drāviḍa and vesara types

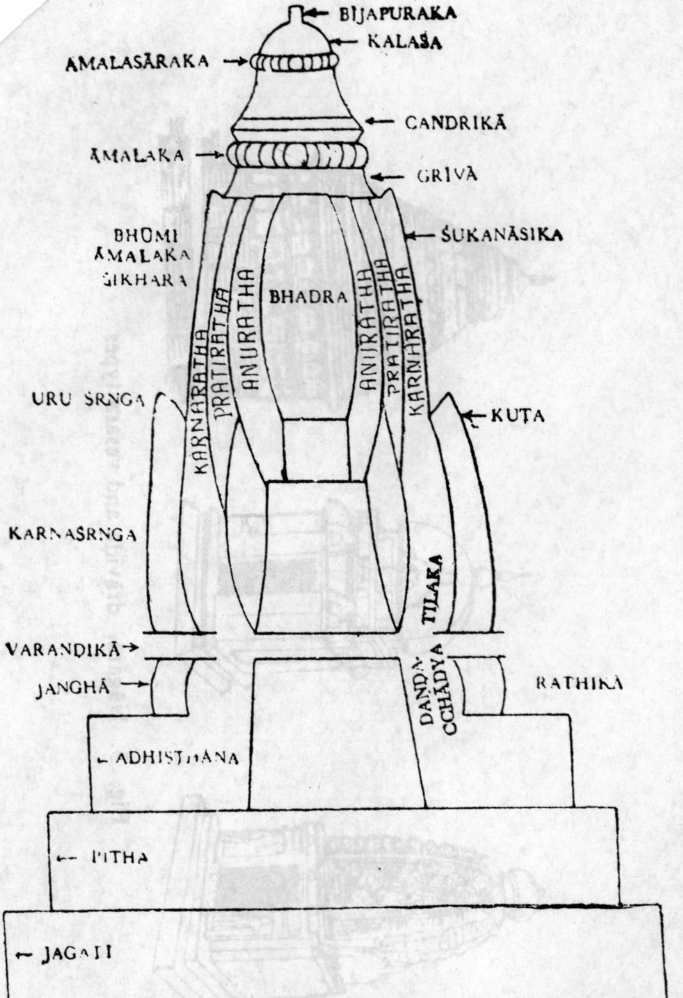

A TEMPLE SKETCH—REPRESENTING PRINCIPAL TERMS.

Fig. 4. Details of a śikhara (Orissa type)

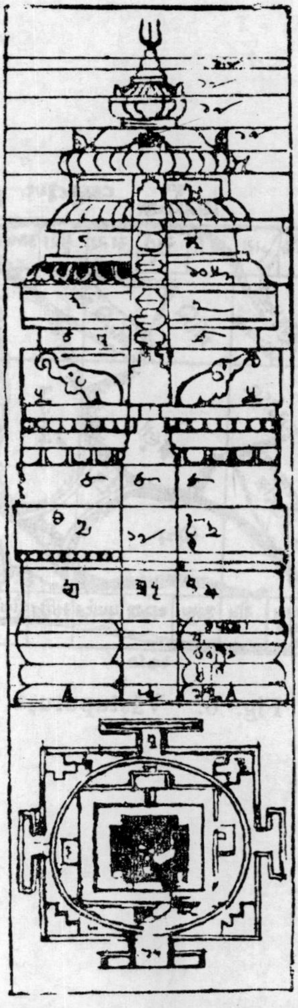

Fig. 5. Plan and elevation of a temple based on a maṇḍala

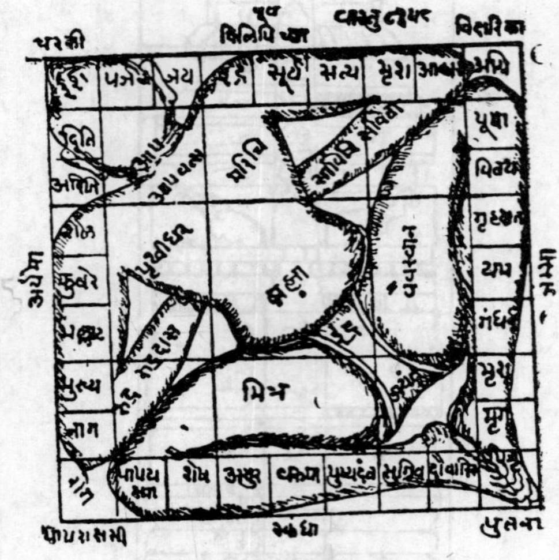

Fig. 6. Vāstupuruṣa

Fig. 6. (A) A Coronar sectiony through a pratiṣṭa showing Ṣaḍādhāra pratiṣṭha

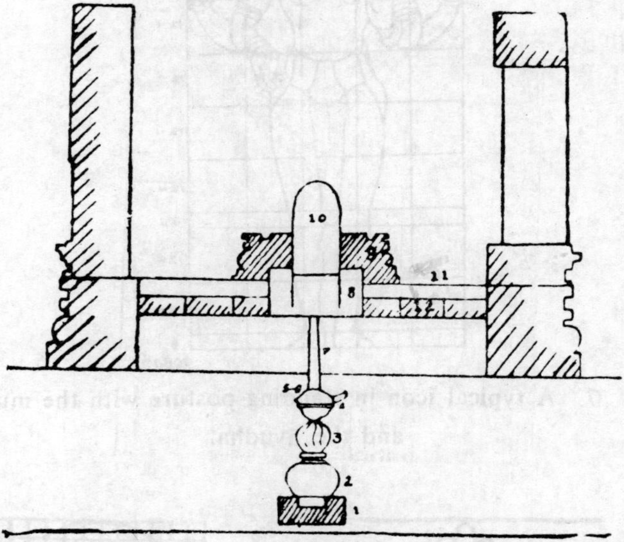

1. Ādhāraśilā 2. Nidhikumbha 3. Padma 4. Kūrma 5. Place for silver lotus and kūrma 6. Place for gold lotus and kūrma 7. Yoganālī 8. Napuṁsakaśilā 9. Pīṭha 10. Vigraha 11. Floor of garbhagṛha 12. Iṣṭakā-cayana

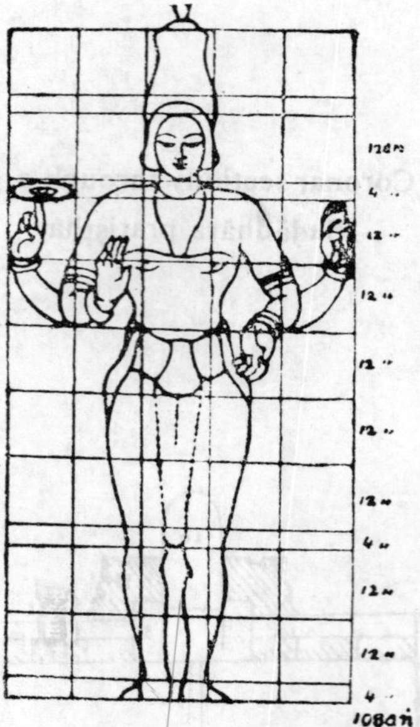

Fig 7. A typical icon in standing posture with the mudrā and the āyudha.

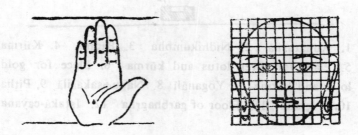

Fig. 8. Tālamāna system with the measurement of the palm and the face as a fundamental unit.

Fig. 9. A typical ratha (temple car used for processions)

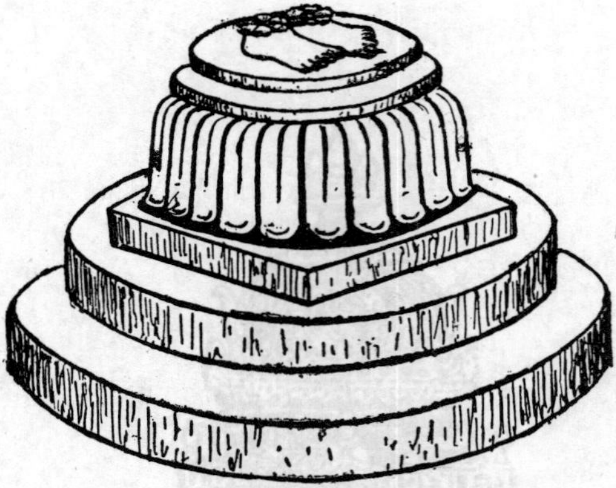

Fig. 11. Balipīṭha

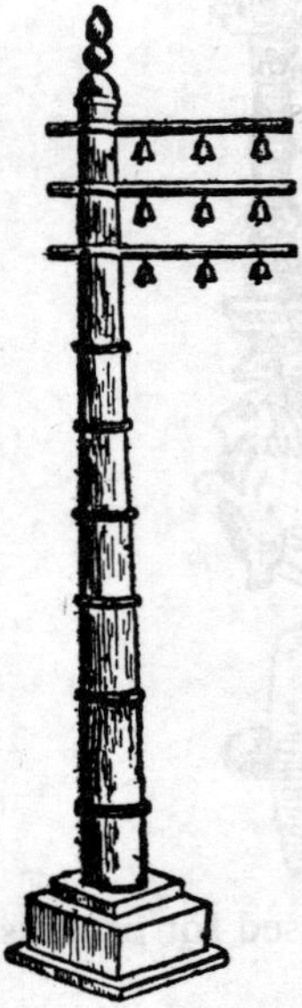

Fig. 10. Dhvajastaṁbha

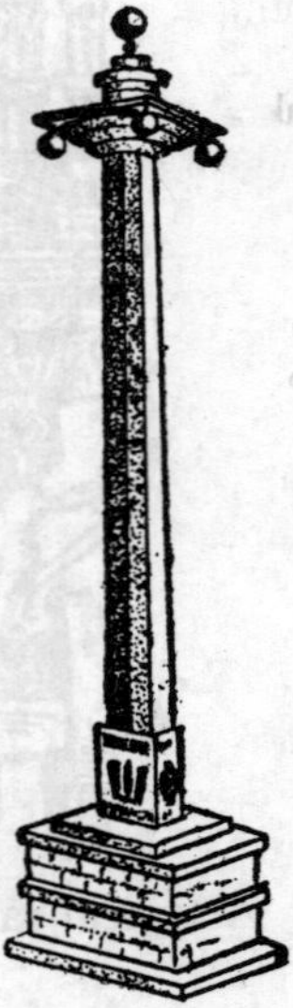

Fig. 12. Dīpastaṁbha

INDEX

A

Abharana (Ornaments) 24
Abhayamudra 25
Abhiseka 29
Adhisthanapitha 12
Adhivasa ceremonies 27
Agamas 5
Agamasastra 38
Aihole 5
Aihole Temples, N.K. 4
Aksimocana 17
Alampur, A.P. 5
All India Temple Trust 38
Amalasara 12
Anahata cakra 14
Andhra Pradesh 36
Anghri 13
Angkor 9
Ankurarpana 17
Ankusa 25
Antarala 21
Antaryamin 14
Apsidal chapels 5
Arabia 36
Arcavatara 32
Architecture 2
Architecture - northern style 3
Architecture - southern style 3
Ardhamantapa 11
Asanas 24, 25
Astabandha 27
Astrology 31
Atharvaveda 23
Avabhrtha-snana 28
Avahana 30

B

Babylonia 35
Balipitha, Illus. 52
Balis 26
Bana 25
Banteay Srei Temple 9
Being 1
Belur 8
Bengal 8
Besakh of Bali 9
Bhajans 40
Bheritadana 30
Bhuloka 11
Bhumara, M P 3
Bhuvarloka 12
Brhadisvara temple 7
Brhat Samhita 5
Brahmaloka 12
Brahmanas 36
Brahmanical 4
Brahmasila 18
Brahmotsava 29
Buddhist 5
Buddhist Shrines 4

C

Cakras 14, 25
Calacala 24

Calukyan style 7
Calukyas 5
Calukyas of Badami 4
Cambodia 9
Candesvara 22
Carana 13
Cave temples 2
Central India 8
Chandellas 8
Chen La Temple 9
Christianity 39
Church 2, 39
Cihna (symbol) 24
Circular plan 5
Colas 6, 7
Cola temples 7
Cosmic Law 1
Cosmic Power 1
Cyprus 36

D

Daivapacaras 32
Damaru 25
Dance 34
Dasara 29
Deccan (Western) 5
Deogarh, UP 3
Devadasis 35, 36
Devalaya 2, 9
Devi Temple 21
Dhanyadhivasa 27
Dharma 34
Dhruvabera 24
Dhvajarohana 30
Dhvajastambha, Illus. 52
Dhvajastambha 10, 21, 22, 32
Dieng 8
Dipastambha, Ills. 52
Dipastambha 23
Dravida 3, 5, 6
Dravidian Architecture 4, 6
Dravidian tradition 7
Durga temple 4, 22

E

Egypt 36
Epic literature 13

F

Face (measurement Talamana system) Illus. 50

G

Gada 25
Gala or Griva (Neck) 13
Ganapati 22
Garbhagrha 10, 11, 14, 15, 18, 20, 21, 24, 29
Garbhanyasa 18
Garuda 21, 22
God 1
Gopurams 7, 10, 12, 22
Granaries 35
Greece 36
Griva 13

Gujarat 6, 8
Gupta Period 3

H

Halebid 8
Hampi 7
Hanuman 22
Harikathas 34, 40
Hinduising 40
Hinduism 40
Hindus 37, 39
Hindu pantheon 17
Hindu Religion 10
Hindu Society 37, 41, 42
Hindu Temples 24, 33
Homakunda 26, 27
Hospitals and dispensaries 35
Hoysalas 7
Huchimalligudi 4

I

Icon in standing posture,
Illus. 50
Iconography 23
Idong Songo 8
Islam 39

J

Jabalpur M P 3
Jagannatha 24
Jagannatha Temple 8
Jain 4
Jaladhivasa 27
Janaloka 12
Jangha (Shank) 13
Japa 29
Java 8

K

Kailasanatha Temple 6
Kailasanatha temple (Ellora) 4
Kalasa 11, 14, 26, 28
Kancheepuram 6
Kantha 13
Karna 13
Karnataka 7, 36
Karnataka, North 4
Karnataka, South 5
Kasinatha temple 4
Kerala 8
Khadga 25
Khajuraho, M P 8, 13
Konarak (Orissa) 13
Kumbhabhiseka 28

L

Ladkhan temple 4
Lakshmi 22
Lanchana 21
Lara Jonggrang 9
Lingaraja Temple 8
Lion 21
Lotus 18

M

Madurai 7
Mahabalipuram 6
Maharloka 12
Maharashtra 36
Majapahit dynasty 9
Mandala 14, 15, 17
Manipura 14
Marriage 41, 42
Masjid 2
Meruparvata 12
Mesapotamia 36
Mosques 39
Mt. Abu 8
Mudras 24, 25
Mukhamantapa 20, 21
Muladhara 14
Murdhestaka 17
Music 34
Mythological literature 13

N

Nachna (Rajasthan) 3
Nagara 3, 5, 6
Nagara, dravida and Vesara
types, Illus. 45
Naimittika-puja 29
Nandi 21
Nasika (nose) 13, 14
Navatala 25
Nayaks 6
Nayaks of Madurai 7
Netronmilana 26
Nidhikumbha 18
Nityapuja 28
Nrttamantapa
(or Navaranga) 11, 21

O

Orissa 6, 8

P

Pada (Foot) 13
Padma 25
Padmasana 25
Paduka 13
Pakasala 23
Palm (measurement
Talamana system)
Illus. 50
Pallavas 4, 6
Pampapati temple 7
Panataran (Java) 9
Panda - Psychology 39
Pandyans 7
Pandyas 4, 6
Papanatha temple 4
Parivaradevatas 22
Partisthavidhi 26
Parvati 22
Pasa 25
Pattadakal temples 4, 5
Pilgrimage 10
Pradaksinapatha 20
Prakara 10, 11, 22
Pranbanan 9

Pranapratistha 27
Prasada 10
Prasadas (or vimanas) 6
Prastara 12
Pravacanas 34
Priests 38
Prostitution 36
Pancaloha 24
Puja vessels 31
Puranas 5, 12
Puri 24
Puskarini 23, 32
Pyramid 3, 6

R

Rastrakutas 4
Ratha, Illus. 51
Ratha 6, 24, 27, 30
Ratha etching 31
Rathotsava 29, 30
Rajasthan 6, 8
Religion 34
Rgveda 23
Rock-cut temples 4

S

Sadadhara Pratistha, Illus. 49
Sahasrara 14
Sailendra Dynasty 8
Saiva 24
Saiva and Sakta 25
Sakta 24
Sakti 24
Sambor Prei Kuk 9
Samsara 11
Sanchi 3
Sanctum sanctorum 10, 20
Sangamesvara temple 4
Sankalpa 16
Sankha 25
Satyaloka 12
Sayana 24
Sayyadhivasa 27
Sculpture 2, 6
Sikha 11, 12, 13
Sikhara (Orissa type) Illus. 46
Sikhara 11, 12, 19
Sikhara area 14
Silanyasa 18
Sira 13
Sirsa 13
Siva 22, 24
Siva and Sakti 10
Sivaratri 29
Siva temple 8, 21, 22
Solankis 8
Soma 17
Somanathapura 8
South East Asia 8, 36
South India 4
Srirangam 7
Stambhas 12
Stellar plan 5
Sthanaka 24
Sthapaka or Acarya 16
Sthapati (Architect) 16, 28

Stupika 12
Subrahmanya 22
Sukanasi (or Ardhamantapa) 11, 20, 21
Surya Temple 8
Surya Temple at Modhera 8
Surya Varman II 9
Sutragrahin (Surveyor) 16
Sutras 5
Svadhisthana 14
Svargabrahma temple 5
Svarloka 12
Symbology 9, 14
Synagogue 2
Syria 36

T

Taksaka (Sculptor) 16
Tala 25
Tamil Nadu 4, 36
Tampaksiring of Bali 9
Tantric Literature 5
Tantricism 13
Tapoloka 12
Temple 2
Temple based on mandala, Illus. 47
Tenoke cinokex (Ground plan) Illus. 43
Temple of Simple design (Illus.) 44
Terracotta 8
Tigawa 3
Tirtha 10
Tortoise 18
Trisula 25

U

Upacaras 29
Upper India 6
Uru 13
Utsavamurti 23, 29, 30

V

Vahana 21
Vaikuntha Ekadasi 29
Vaikuntha Perumal Temple 6
Vaisnava 24
Vaisnava Images 25
Varadamudra 25
Vardhakin (Builder) 16
Vasana (dress) 24
Vastumandala 16
Vastupurusa, Illus. 48
Vastupurusa 17, 26
Vastu Sastra 5
Vastuvinyasa 16
Vedic age 2
Vedic Mantras 2
Vesara 3, 5
Vesara Temple 20
Vijayanagar 6, 7
Vijayanagar kings 6
Vimana 5, 7, 8
Vindhyan uplands 6
Virupaksa temple 5
Visnu 24

Visnu Temple 21, 22
Visuddha and ajna cakras 14
Vitthala Temple 7
Voltaire 1

W

Worship - place of 1

Y

Yagasala 2, 23, 26, 27, 28, 30
Yajamana 16
Yoganala 18
Yogasana 25